STECK-VAUGHN

Comprehension Skills

FACTS

LEVEL
D

Linda Ward Beech
Tara McCarthy
Donna Townsend

STECK-VAUGHN
COMPANY
A Subsidiary of National Education Corporation

Executive Editor:	Diane Sharpe
Project Editor:	Melinda Veatch
Senior Editor:	Anne Rose Souby
Design Coordinator:	Sharon Golden
Project Design:	Howard Adkins Communications
Cover Illustration:	Rhonda Childress
Photographs:	©Philippe Blondel / Photo Researchers

ISBN 0-8114-7843-2

6 7 8 9 10 VP 03 02 01 00 99 98

Facts are things like names, dates, and places. In this book you will practice finding facts.

What is happening in the picture on this page? Where is this action taking place? What is the person wearing? The answers to these questions are facts. What other facts can you find in the picture?

What Are Facts?

Facts are sometimes called details. They are small pieces of information. Facts can appear in true stories, such as those in the newspaper. They can also appear in legends and other stories that people make up.

How to Read for Facts

You can find facts by asking yourself questions. Ask *who*, and your answer will be a fact about a person. Ask *what*, and your answer will be a fact about a thing. Ask *where*, and your answer will be a fact about a place. Ask *when*, and your answer will be a fact about a time. Ask *how many* or *how much*, and your answer will be a fact about a number or an amount.

Try It!

Read this story and look for facts as you read. Ask yourself *what* and *when*.

◆

The *Titanic*

On April 10, 1912, the *Titanic* left England on its first trip. It was the largest and one of the safest ships ever built. Many rich and famous people were on board. They planned to arrive in New York in six days. But on the night of April 14, the ship ran into an iceberg. The iceberg tore a huge hole in the ship's side. The passengers climbed into lifeboats as the ship began to sink. But there were not enough boats for everyone. Only 711 of the 2,207 people on board lived to tell about the shipwreck.

Did you find these facts when you read the paragraph? Write the facts on the lines below.

◆ What happened to the *Titanic*?

Fact: _____

◆ When did the ship run into the iceberg?

Fact: _____

To check your answers, turn to page 62.

Practice Finding Facts

Below are some practice questions. The first two are already answered. You can do the third one on your own.

_B_   **1.** How many people lived to tell about the shipwreck?

     A. 2,207   **c.** 500

     B. 711   **D.** 947

Look at the question and answers again. The words *how many* are asking for a number. There are many numbers in the paragraph, but you are looking for one that tells how many people lived through the disaster. Read the paragraph until you find the words *lived to tell about the shipwreck*. The sentence says that only 711 of the 2,207 people on board lived. So the correct answer is **B**.

_C_   **2.** The *Titanic* was sailing to

     A. England   **c.** New York

     B. Paris   **D.** Iceland

Look at the question. It asks for the name of the place the *Titanic* was sailing to. Search the story for the names of places. You should find this sentence: "They planned to arrive in New York in six days." So the correct answer is **c**.

Now it's your turn to practice. Answer the next question by writing the letter of the correct answer on the line.

_____   **3.** When did the *Titanic* leave England?

     A. April 10, 1912   **c.** June 4, 1912

     B. March 1, 1912   **D.** April 14, 1912

To check your answer, turn to page 62.

Using What You Know

Read the following question words and facts that answer the questions. Ask yourself the questions. Then write facts about yourself on the lines.

Who?

George Washington was the first president of the United States.
Richard Byrd made five trips to Antarctica.

◆ My name is _____.

What?

Parts of the ivy plant are poisonous.
Some seals can dive very deep.

◆ My favorite animal is _____.

Where?

Most tigers live in Asia.
Hawaii is about two thousand miles southwest of San Francisco.

◆ I live in the city of _____.

When?

School begins at 7:45.
Baseball starts in the spring.

◆ I was born on _____,19 ____.

How Many?/How Much?

A foot has twelve inches.
A large catcus can hold a ton of water.

◆ There are _____ students in my class.

How to Use This Book

In this book you will read 25 stories. Each story has two parts. Read the first part, then answer five questions about it. Then read the second part, and answer the next five questions.

You can check your answers by looking at pages 59 through 61. Write the number of correct answers in the score box at the top of the page. After you finish all the stories, turn to pages 56 through 58. Work through "Think and Apply." The answers to those questions are on page 62.

Remember

This book asks questions about facts in stories. When you answer the questions, use the facts in the story. You may already know some facts about the subject. But the story will have the answers you need for the questions.

Hints for Better Reading

◆ Look for facts while you are reading the stories. Notice the names of people, animals, and things. Look for places, dates, and times.

◆ Read each question carefully. Think about the facts you need to answer the question. Try to find a sentence in the story that has some of the same words as the question.

◆ Try to remember the facts you read in the story. If you can't remember, look back at the story.

Challenge Yourself

Try this special challenge. Read each story. Cover the story with a sheet of paper. Try to remember the facts. Answer the questions without looking back at the story.

How do you know that spring is on its way? For many Americans the first sign of spring is baseball. In late winter many big league teams head south. They go to training camps in warm states such as Florida and Arizona. There they get ready for the opening of baseball season in early April.

Each team has its own camp. The players spend long days training and getting in shape. They run, hit, throw, and catch. They learn to listen to the coaches and to work together as a team. They also play some practice games against other teams. These are called exhibition games.

Spring training camps are full of hope. New players hope to stay on the team. Other players hope to have their best baseball season. Everyone hopes to be part of a winning team.

_____ **1.** For many people baseball is a sign of
  A. season   **C.** spring
  B. work   **D.** winter

_____ **2.** Players go to training camps in Florida and
  A. Arizona   **C.** April
  B. Arkansas   **D.** Americans

_____ **3.** The players run, hit, throw, and
  A. coach   **C.** camp
  B. catch   **D.** kick

_____ **4.** Practice games are called
  A. spring training   **C.** spring games
  B. winning records   **D.** exhibition games

_____ **5.** Spring training camps are full of
  A. hope   **C.** trees
  B. bats   **D.** fans

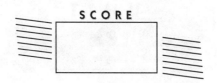
What do baseball teams pack when they go south? The list is very long! One team from New York takes 3,600 baseballs, 360 bats, 200 uniforms, and 75 helmets. Baseball teams also take pitching machines. Many teams take trunks full of medicine and bandages.

Each player also packs things for the trip. Some take bicycles, golf clubs, and beach chairs. Others take their own television sets. Players taking their children might pack toys and games.

Large vans move the teams to their training camps. Many helpers load and unload the equipment and baggage. By April it's time to move again. The baseball season has begun.

_____ **6.** One team takes along thousands of
    A. helmets   **C.** baseballs
    B. uniforms   **D.** machines

_____ **7.** Baseball teams take machines that
    A. catch   **C.** patch
    B. jog   **D.** pitch

_____ **8.** Players sometimes take their own
    A. bikes   **C.** beds
    B. teams   **D.** boats

_____ **9.** The teams move to training camps in big
    A. planes   **C.** vans
    B. cabs   **D.** workers

_____ **10.** Loading and unloading the trucks takes many
    A. days   **C.** machines
    B. weeks   **D.** helpers

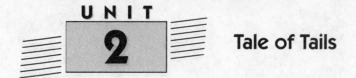

U N I T 2

Tale of Tails

Many animals have tails. They use their tails for many different purposes. For instance, some animals use their tails as fly swatters. Have you ever seen a cow flicking its tail back and forth? It's getting rid of bugs. Horses use their tails in this way, too.

Some animals hang by their tails. Monkeys often do this. Then they can use all four of their paws for other things, such as eating. Another animal that uses its tail as a "hanger" is the opossum. The opossum also uses its tail to help it climb trees.

Animals that live in the water use their tails to help them swim. A fish moves its tail from side to side. The rest of its body curves in the opposite direction from its tail. Alligators and crocodiles also swing their tails as they swim. Their large tails give them power and speed.

_____ **1.** Animals use their tails for different
    A. periods   **C.** seasons
    B. purposes   **D.** lengths

_____ **2.** An animal that uses its tail as a fly swatter is the
    A. cow   **C.** hog
    B. fish   **D.** bug

_____ **3.** The monkey uses its tail to
    A. swim   **C.** hang
    B. climb   **D.** talk

_____ **4.** A fish moves its tail
    A. up and down   **C.** in a circle
    B. from side to side   **D.** upside down

_____ **5.** Alligators and crocodiles use their tails for
    A. fishing   **C.** power
    B. flying   **D.** curves

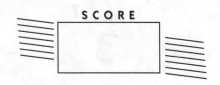
The kangaroo has a large, useful tail. It is like a chair. The kangaroo leans on its tail to rest. The tail is also good for leaping and landing. It helps the kangaroo keep its balance. This is important because an adult kangaroo can leap as far as 15 feet at a time.

A fox has a big, bushy tail. This is a good tail to have on cold nights. The fox can put its tail over its nose and paws while it sleeps. The tail is a blanket that keeps the fox warm.

Some animals don't keep their tails with them at all times. One example is the lizard. If an enemy pulls the lizard's tail in a struggle, the tail breaks off. The lizard leaves its tail and runs to safety. Don't worry! The lizard will soon grow a new tail.

_____

_____ 6. The kangaroo uses its tail as a place to
    A. eat   C. lean
    B. grow   D. leave

_____ 7. A kangaroo's tail is also helpful for
    A. jumping   C. walking
    B. swimming   D. crying

_____ 8. The fox uses its bushy tail as a
    A. pillow   C. chair
    B. cover   D. brush

_____ 9. A lizard's tail can help the lizard escape from
    A. friends   C. enemies
    B. kangaroos   D. blankets

_____ 10. The lizard can grow a new
    A. fin   C. nose
    B. leg   D. tail

The summer night is quiet. Then suddenly strange, hooting sounds drift through the dark. It seems as if huge owls are flying through the night sky or standing tall on the limbs of trees.

It may be that the hoots are really made by baby birds, or fledglings, that are still in their nest. They are young great horned owls.

Great horned owls have a very long childhood. Most other young birds leave their nests two or three weeks after they hatch. When great horned owls hatch in the early spring, they are blind and helpless. Their parents must take care of them completely for more than two months. When the young owls get hungry at night, they hoot to their parents for food.

_____ 1. On a summer night, you may hear hoots that seem
  A. dark   C. quiet
  B. bright   D. strange

_____ 2. Fledglings are
  A. owl nests   C. adult owls
  B. baby birds   D. cries for food

_____ 3. After three weeks most young birds
  A. hatch   C. leave their nests
  B. hoot for food D. are blind

_____ 4. The young owl's parents must
  A. care for them C. give them lessons
  B. fly away   D. make noises

_____ 5. The little owls hoot when they
  A. sit on trees   C. go to sleep
  B. get hungry   D. become frightened

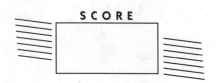
The little horned owls grow up to have very keen vision. Unlike some birds, their eyes are set like human eyes. They look directly forward. They see well in all kinds of light. Even in the dim light of a candle, an owl sees things that are a thousand feet away.

An owl has special soft flight feathers all around the edges of its wings. When air brushes through these feathers, there is no sound at all. So, the owl can silently swoop down to catch a mouse or an insect.

When the cool weather of autumn comes, the young owls leave the nest. Their bodies and wings are strong. At last they are ready to live on their own.

_____ **6.** An owl's eyes look
- **A.** sideways
- **B.** dimly
- **C.** ahead
- **D.** warmly

_____ **7.** An owl can see
- **A.** without much light
- **B.** itself
- **C.** vision
- **D.** silently

_____ **8.** The flight feathers help owls
- **A.** move quietly
- **B.** fly quickly
- **C.** grow fast
- **D.** brush air

_____ **9.** Owls like to catch
- **A.** faint sounds
- **B.** mice and bugs
- **C.** rustling leaves
- **D.** big claws

_____ **10.** When fall arrives, young owls are
- **A.** with their parents
- **B.** still learning
- **C.** feeling cold
- **D.** on their own

Most people in the United States speak English. But they don't use the same words for the same things. For instance, what do you call a round, flat breakfast food served with maple syrup? Some people call these *flapjacks*. In other places people call them *griddlecakes*. If you live in the hills of Arkansas or Tennessee, you might answer *flitters*. If you live in Mississippi, you might say *battercakes*. Or, like most people in the United States, you might say *pancakes*.

Suppose you are talking about an insect some people call a *dragonfly*. People in Florida wouldn't know what that means. They call this insect a *mosquito hawk*. But people in nearby Georgia don't know what a mosquito hawk is. They call the very same insect a *snake doctor*! Still another word for dragonfly is *snake feeder*.

_____ **1.** People describe things using different
     A. works   **C.** plants
     B. words   **D.** sights

_____ **2.** A dragonfly is a kind of
     A. insect   **C.** doctor
     B. pancake   **D.** monster

_____ **3.** Another word that means flapjack is
     A. carrot cake   **C.** griddlecake
     B. dragonfly   **D.** slapjack

_____ **4.** A dragonfly is also called a
     A. snake doctor   **C.** snake nurse
     B. snakeroot   **D.** snapdragon

_____ **5.** The word *mosquito hawk* is used by people in
     A. Oregon   **C.** Tennessee
     B. Arkansas   **D.** Florida

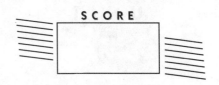
Do you want to build a fire? Building a fire might not be very easy if you live in the United States. One language expert has found 169 different words for the wood used to start a fire. Some of these words are *lighterd knots, kindling wood,* and *lightning wood.*

Let's go shopping. Do you want cling peaches, plum peaches, green peaches, or pickle peaches? It doesn't matter. They are all the same thing. It just depends on where you are.

Once you buy your fruit, you can put it in a paper bag, a sack, or even a poke. You can eat it at home on your porch, veranda, or gallery. You might want to invite your friend or buddy to share the snack, chow, or grub. Don't eat the pits, though. They will make you sick no matter what you call them!

_____ **6.** You use kindling wood to
    A. build a porch   **C.** build a house
    B. start a fire   **D.** plant trees

_____ **7.** A poke is a
    A. paper   **C.** sack
    B. plum   **D.** pig

_____ **8.** How many words mean the same as *lighterd knots*?
    A. 196   **C.** 16
    B. 168   **D.** 96

_____ **9.** A green peach is the same as a
    A. cling peach   **C.** red plum
    B. pink peach   **D.** green plum

_____ **10.** Some Americans say *gallery* instead of
    A. porch   **C.** kitchen
    B. pooch   **D.** vessel

A story tells that long ago the sun and the storm were sister and brother. Sun Woman heated the earth and made crops grow. People welcomed her golden light. Storm Man was not so welcome! People hid from his dark clouds and loud thunder.

There came a time when Storm Man made the mightiest storm ever. Lightning bolts struck the earth, and rushing water covered the fields. The storm was so terrifying that everyone hid. Moon Woman and all the stars found shelter behind the Milky Way.

Finally Storm Man grew weary, and he ended the storm. People crept out of their houses. Moon Woman and the stars cautiously moved back into the sky. But Sun Woman did not come back. The earth grew cold, and crops died in the fields. People shivered and wept, and even Storm Man grew worried. Where was his sister? He went to Moon Woman to find an answer.

_____ **1.** People welcomed Sun Woman's
  A. light   **C.** brother
  B. crops   **D.** gold

_____ **2.** Storm Man caused people to
  A. rain   **C.** boom
  B. warm up   **D.** run away

_____ **3.** During the greatest storm, everyone
  A. hid   **C.** covered their fields
  B. fled to the sky **D.** played

_____ **4.** Sun Woman did not return, so Storm Man grew
  A. angry   **C.** colder
  B. happy   **D.** worried

_____ **5.** Storm Man went to Moon Woman to
  A. get warm   **C.** find an answer
  B. laugh   **D.** shiver

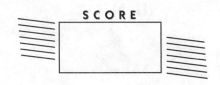
Moon Woman knew that Sun Woman was very frightened. She also knew that something unusual could make Sun Woman leave that dark cave. Moon Woman had an idea. She asked Dance Girl to perform a special dance.

At the dark cave where Sun Woman was hiding, Dance Girl began. She hopped, flopped, and waggled her head. She rolled her eyes and flapped her arms. This was the funniest dance the world had ever seen! Moon Woman and all the stars laughed. Even the people forgot about the cold and laughed as they watched Dance Girl.

Inside her cave Sun Woman heard the world's laughter and became curious. She peeped out and started laughing. She moved out into the sky to get a better view. And from that day on, Sun Woman has never deserted the sky again.

_____

_____ **6.** Sun Woman stayed in the cave because she was
- **A.** lost
- **B.** scared
- **C.** angry
- **D.** strange

_____ **7.** Moon Woman wanted to
- **A.** do another dance
- **B.** share a secret
- **C.** make Sun Woman curious
- **D.** find something

_____ **8.** Dance Girl's dance was
- **A.** funny
- **B.** beautiful
- **C.** useless
- **D.** sad

_____ **9.** As they watched Dance Girl, people began to
- **A.** cry
- **B.** clap
- **C.** perform
- **D.** laugh

_____ **10.** Sun Woman went out into the sky to
- **A.** help the world
- **B.** join her friends
- **C.** see the dance better
- **D.** peep out of the cave

The game of jump rope is hundreds of years old. It is played in countries around the world. In most places all you need is a rope and some people. If you live in Hungary, you might use twisted straw instead of rope. Some children in Spain use strips of leather. Long, strong vines make good jump ropes, too.

Jump rope players in Greece use elastic instead of rope. The players loop the elastic around their ankles. The jumper has to move in and out of the elastic without touching it. This version of the game takes much skill.

One of the trickiest jump rope games is called Double Dutch. In this game players turn two ropes at the same time. When the ropes are turned fast, the players call it pepper. Some cities in the United States hold Double Dutch contests. Then the ropes are turned very fast. This is called hot pepper!

_____ 1. Players in Hungary sometimes use
- A. leather strips
- B. twisted ropes
- C. twisted straw
- D. plastic strips

_____ 2. Good jump ropes can be made from long, strong
- A. straw
- B. vines
- C. pipes
- D. veins

_____ 3. Players in Greece use
- A. vines
- B. their arms
- C. rubber bands
- D. elastic

_____ 4. Players use two ropes in
- A. the United Kingdom
- B. Double Dutch
- C. Double Spain
- D. Hungary

_____ 5. When the ropes are turned fast, players call it
- A. pepper
- B. piper
- C. salt
- D. sugar

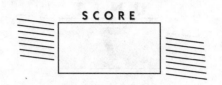

Jump rope has long been a game of fun. But jumping rope has a more serious side. People of all ages are jumping rope for exercise.

Many athletes jump rope to warm up for a sport. Others do it as part of their daily workout. Jumping keeps their muscles strong and active. It is a good way to stay in shape.

People who do not like activities such as running often jump rope. Jumping for ten minutes is about the same as running one mile. Some people do their jumping in gyms. Others do it in their homes or even in their offices.

Jumping rope is a popular exercise because it's good for your health. Doctors say that jumping rope can improve the way the heart and lungs work. It might even help people live longer.

_____ **6.** Many athletes jump rope
    A. every day   **C.** monthly
    B. early   **D.** slowly

_____ **7.** Jumping rope is a good way to stay
    A. fat   **C.** cold
    B. healthy   **D.** fun

_____ **8.** Some people jump rope because they don't like to
    A. hop   **C.** run
    B. toss   **D.** ski

_____ **9.** People jump rope at home and
    A. in bed   **C.** at work
    B. in cars   **D.** at meals

_____ **10.** Jumping rope can improve your
    A. health   **C.** home
    B. work   **D.** wealth

You have probably heard the saying "busy as a beaver." This saying is really true. Beavers are almost always working.

The beaver is a builder. This furry animal builds dams and tunnels. It builds a home called a lodge. The beaver's tools for this work are a broad, flat tail and strong front teeth.

The first thing a beaver does is build a dam. Beavers build their dams across quiet streams where no other beavers live. They use their powerful teeth to cut down trees. Then they use their teeth to make the trees into logs about six feet long. They drag the logs across the stream to the dam. Beavers also use leaves and branches in their dams. They pack them together with mud to make a wall. The beaver's wide tail is handy for slapping the mud into place. When it is finished, the wall of a beaver dam is strong enough to keep out water.

___

_____ 1. Beavers are almost always
  A. playing   C. sleeping
  B. working   D. fighting

_____ 2. A beaver home is called a
  A. cabin   C. lodge
  B. dam   D. ledge

_____ 3. Beavers build dams across quiet
  A. puddles   C. streets
  B. oceans   D. streams

_____ 4. Beavers cut down trees with their
  A. paws   C. saws
  B. teeth   D. tails

_____ 5. Beavers pack the branches in their dams with
  A. clay   C. glue
  B. water   D. mud

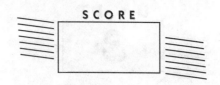
The beaver's dam holds back the water in the stream. A pond forms behind the dam. Then the beaver builds its lodge in the middle of the pond. This is the beaver's way of keeping its home safe from other animals.

Most of a beaver's lodge is under the water. The beaver dives under the water to get to the entrance. Then it swims through tunnels to get to the upper part of the lodge. This part of the lodge is above the water. It is a safe place where the beaver can raise a family.

The inside of a beaver's lodge is hollow. Here the beavers raise a family. They have as many as six young in April or May. Young beavers stay with their parents until they are two years old. Then they leave the lodge to find a new stream and begin their busy adult lives.

_____ **6.** Beavers build homes in the middle of ponds for
    A. fun   **C.** protest
    B. protection   **D.** enjoyment

_____ **7.** The entrance is
    A. very large   **C.** under the water
    B. under the ground **D.** above the water

_____ **8.** The beaver swims through the entrance into
    A. stairs   **C.** tunnels
    B. mines   **D.** enemies

_____ **9.** The upper part of the lodge is
    A. on the banks   **C.** under the water
    B. behind the water **D.** out of the water

_____ **10.** Beavers have as many as
    A. six young   **C.** eight young
    B. seven young   **D.** ten young

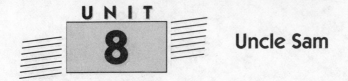
Uncle Sam is a symbol. He stands for the government and people of the United States. He is dressed in clothes of red, white, and blue. He wears a hat with stars and stripes on it. These are the colors and designs of the American flag.

No one is sure how the name *Uncle Sam* got started. The first time the name appeared in print was in 1813. It caught on and was soon used in other places. In 1830 a picture of Uncle Sam was used in a cartoon. You can still find him in cartoons today.

The United States Army has used Uncle Sam on many of its posters. The most famous poster shows Uncle Sam pointing his finger. He is saying, "I want you." This poster first appeared in 1917. America was fighting in World War I. The poster urged people to join the Army.

_____ **1.** Uncle Sam is a United States
    A. relative   **C.** athlete
    B. symbol   **D.** officer

_____ **2.** Uncle Sam wears the colors of the American
    A. flower   **C.** army
    B. eagle   **D.** flag

_____ **3.** The words *Uncle Sam* first appeared in print in
    A. 1917   **C.** 1830
    B. 1813   **D.** 1381

_____ **4.** You can still find Uncle Sam in
    A. cartoons   **C.** movies
    B. stories   **D.** factories

_____ **5.** The United States Army has used Uncle Sam on
    A. uniforms   **C.** books
    B. costumes   **D.** posters

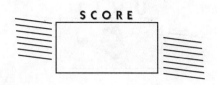
The most popular story of how Uncle Sam began is based on a tale about a man named Samuel Wilson. Sam Wilson lived in Troy, New York, in the early 1800s. He was a jolly man who had many friends. People sometimes called him Uncle Sam.

In 1812 the United States was at war with Great Britain. During this war Sam Wilson checked barrels of salted meat for the soldiers at a nearby fort. These barrels had the letters *U.S.* stamped on them. The letters stood for *United States*.

The soldiers from around Troy knew Sam Wilson. When he checked the meat, they made jokes. They said it was "Uncle Sam's meat." Other soldiers who did not know Sam Wilson got mixed up. They thought the *U.S.* on the barrels stood for *Uncle Sam*. And that is how the name got started.

_____ 6. Sam Wilson was called Uncle Sam because he was
    A. unhappy   **C.** friendly
    B. lonely   **D.** selfish

_____ 7. Sam Wilson's job was
    A. telling stories   **C.** checking meat
    B. fighting enemies   **D.** making barrels

_____ 8. On the barrels were two
    A. letters   **C.** numbers
    B. pictures   **D.** soldiers

_____ 9. The soldiers from Troy joked that *U.S.* meant
    A. United States   **C.** Uncle Sam
    B. Uncle Sid   **D.** United Sam

_____ 10. The soldiers who did not know Sam Wilson were
    A. checked   **C.** amused
    B. confused   **D.** hungry

Long ago the Tewa people were homeless. Everywhere they went, enemies destroyed their houses and fields. "Where can we go?" the discouraged Tewa cried. Then Long Sash had an idea. "If you follow me," said Long Sash, "I will take you to the Middle Place where we can live in peace. But I warn you, the journey will seem like an endless trail. Many of you will suffer and grow weary, and some of you may even die on the way." The Tewa pleaded, "Take us on this journey. We trust you completely, Long Sash, and we will follow you to the Middle Place."

So the Tewa began their journey. They traveled for many years, and they grew weary. As they became discouraged, they often quarreled among themselves. Finally Long Sash said angrily, "These quarrels are harmful. Shall we stop now? We will call this the Place of Decision. Decide if you want to journey on to the Middle Place." The Tewa decided to go on with Long Sash.

_____ **1.** Enemies destroyed the Tewa's
  A. people   C. houses
  B. leaders   D. food

_____ **2.** Long Sash wanted the Tewa to
  A. rescue him   C. warn him
  B. follow him   D. show him

_____ **3.** Long Sash said that the journey would seem like
  A. an endless trail   C. the Middle Place
  B. a holiday   D. the Place of Decision

_____ **4.** Long Sash thought that quarrels were
  A. harmful   C. necessary
  B. useless   D. silly

_____ **5.** At the Place of Decision, the Tewa
  A. became sick   C. settled down
  B. began their journey D. decided to go on

After many years Long Sash grew old and weary. "You will have to continue without me," he said to the Tewa. "How can we travel to the Middle Place alone?" his people asked him. "We doubt that we can find it." Long Sash replied, "Then we will call this the Place of Doubt." He removed his feathered headdress and gently laid it on the ground. Then he addressed the Tewa again, "When you are in doubt, study the stars. They will guide you to the Middle Place. Two brilliant stars are located over the Place of Decision. My feathered headdress will become a bright cluster of stars above this Place of Doubt. And I myself will travel to the sky where you will see my outline. Even the endless trail will appear in the evening sky. Follow it."

The Tewa were very sad when Long Sash died. But his last words were true. The guiding stars appeared. And the Tewa traveled on to the Middle Place, where they lived forever.

_____

_____ **6.** Long Sash could not lead because he was
  A. lost   **C.** sick
  B. old   **D.** alone

_____ **7.** The Tewa doubted that they could find their
  A. chief   **C.** old map
  B. new home   **D.** feathers

_____ **8.** Two stars were located above the
  A. Place of Doubt   **C.** Place of Decision
  B. Middle Place   **D.** feathered headdress

_____ **9.** The Tewa used the stars to
  A. guide them   **C.** find outlines
  B. tell stories   **D.** cheer them up

_____ **10.** The Tewa finally reached their
  A. doubt   **C.** feather
  B. goal   **D.** leader

Many objects that people use each day started with a simple idea. These objects have often changed the way we live. Some help us to do a job easier. Others fill a need or solve a problem.

In 1858 H. L. Lipman had such an idea. He took out a pencil, a piece of paper, and an eraser. Then he began to write. Sometimes he needed to change a word. Each time he had to search under his books and papers to find the eraser. "I wish my eraser would stay in one place!" he sighed.

Then Lipman had his simple idea. He cut a groove in one end of the pencil. He glued the eraser into this groove. Lipman had solved his problem. Later he thought that others might like to have such a pencil. So he sold his design. Soon pencils with erasers were common. His design earned him $100,000.

_____ **1.** Useful objects often start with
    A. a difficult task   **C.** hard work
    B. a simple idea   **D.** a committee

_____ **2.** Lipman lost his
    A. book   **C.** letter
    B. paper   **D.** eraser

_____ **3.** Lipman glued his eraser
    A. to a pencil   **C.** to a pen
    B. inside a book   **D.** inside his desk

_____ **4.** Lipman thought his idea would
    A. treat an illness   **C.** win a contest
    B. help others   **D.** cause trouble

_____ **5.** When Lipman sold the design, he
    A. made money   **C.** made new friends
    B. became famous   **D.** took a trip

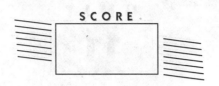
In 1936 Sylvan N. Goldman solved a problem, too. Goldman owned a grocery store. The people who came into his store had to hold the things they needed in their arms as they shopped. Some people could not carry their groceries easily.

Late one night Goldman worked in his small office. He thought about this problem. Then he had an idea. He pushed two folding chairs together so that the seats were touching. He imagined that there was a large basket on the seats. He imagined that there were wheels on the legs of the chairs. "That's it!" he thought. Then he quickly drew his design for the first grocery cart.

Goldman's first cart was made of wood. Later carts were made of metal. The first metal grocery cart is on display at a museum. The cart is displayed with other objects that make life easier for people. Many of these objects started with a simple idea.

_____ 6. Sylvan N. Goldman owned a
A. toy store   C. grocery store
B. drugstore   D. bookstore

_____ 7. The people in Goldman's store had trouble
A. finding things   C. standing in line
B. carrying things   D. paying high prices

_____ 8. Goldman thought about his problem
A. in his office   C. on a train
B. in a museum   D. at home

_____ 9. Goldman had his idea when he looked at
A. his small office   C. erasers
B. Lipman   D. two folding chairs

_____ 10. Goldman's idea made people's lives
A. difficult   C. more interesting
B. happier   D. easier

U N I T
11
Ferris's Wheel

In 1892 Chicago city leaders planned a fair. They wanted it to be the greatest fair ever. It would show the newest ideas in science, business, and art. They also wanted to build something grand at the fair. The Eiffel Tower had been built three years before in France. The Chicago leaders wanted something even grander. So they asked people to send in designs.

G. W. Ferris was a young engineer. He heard about the fair. He designed a huge wheel made of steel. The wheel was 250 feet across. Large cars hung from the end of each spoke. Each car could carry sixty people in a giant circle through the air.

On May 1, 1893, the fair opened. People came from around the world to see the latest inventions. They felt the heat of new electric stoves. They stood in the cool breeze of small fans. They even saw a machine that washed dishes.

_____ 1. Ferris's wheel was
  A. a mile high   C. 250 yards across
  B. 250 feet across   D. 60 feet tall

_____ 2. Ferris's wheel was made of
  A. steel   C. wood
  B. rubber   D. gold

_____ 3. Ferris designed his wheel so people could
  A. walk under it   C. ride it
  B. study it   D. learn about motion

_____ 4. The fair opened
  A. in 1492   C. in 1893
  B. in 1892   D. in 1983

_____ 5. People at the fair felt the heat of
  A. a bonfire   C. a heated fountain
  B. gas heaters   D. electric stoves

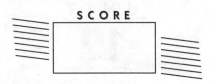
Ferris's wheel was the main attraction at the Chicago fair. People stood in line to ride on it. They wanted to see the fairgrounds from the wheel's highest point. As the wheel cranked upward, some people were frightened. Others were thrilled at what they saw below. Fountains glistened in the sunlight. Flags waved in the breeze. A train snaked through the grounds. At night, colored searchlights lit the sky. Their beams reflected off the water fountains.

When the fair closed, the newspapers called it "a splendid fantasy." Ferris's wheel was later sold for scrap. But today smaller wheels based on his idea turn at fairs all over America. They are called Ferris wheels.

_____ **6.** Ferris's wheel was built
    A. in France   **C.** in Chicago
    B. in Columbus   **D.** beside the Eiffel Tower

_____ **7.** Ferris's wheel
    A. broke down   **C.** was dangerous
    B. was popular   **D.** came from France

_____ **8.** People could ride in Ferris's wheel
    A. only in France   **C.** only in the daytime
    B. only at night   **D.** during the day and night

_____ **9.** Newspapers called the fair a
    A. disaster   **C.** fantasy
    B. failure   **D.** thrill

_____ **10.** Ferris's wheel was sold for scrap
    A. after the fair   **C.** in 1892
    B. before the fair   **D.** during the fair

Tide pools are nature's aquariums. Ocean water flows inland with the tide. The water carries with it many living creatures. The water collects in hollows in rocks and in small holes in the earth. Tide pools are created when the tide goes out. The creatures stay behind in the pools.

Some of the creatures in tide pools seem to sprout from the rocks. They look like plants, but they are simple animals. One of the simplest animals is the sponge. Sponges have no head, mouth, or limbs. They are like blobs of jelly made of tiny cells. Some are bright red. Others are green, brown, or orange. Crabs also live in tide pools. Crabs belong to a group of water animals that have shells. Crabs have special legs shaped like paddles for swimming. Starfish, clams, and sea urchins also live in the tide pools on the seashore.

_____ **1.** Ocean water flows inland with the
    A. pool   **C.** shells
    B. tide   **D.** rocks

_____ **2.** Simple animals can look like
    A. shadows   **C.** crabs
    B. waves   **D.** plants

_____ **3.** One of the simplest animals in a tide pool is
    A. a sponge   **C.** jelly
    B. a rock   **D.** a crab

_____ **4.** Sponges are
    A. simple plants   **C.** different colors
    B. like cracked mud   **D.** like crabs

_____ **5.** Crabs belong to a group of animals with
    A. sponges   **C.** spots
    B. shells   **D.** tails

Tide pools get their life from ocean water. But all the life in the tide pools is in danger from nature's forces. Waves crash into the pools and threaten the life there. The sun's hot rays beat down on the pools. The heat causes the water to dry up slowly. Tides bring more water to some pools. But other pools grow smaller and smaller until they dry into cracked mud.

Most tide pools aren't destroyed by these natural forces. But they are helpless in the face of their greatest enemy—humans. People often collect the animals in the pools. This upsets the balance of nature. Watching the many different animals is fun. But people should not take the animals out of the tide pools.

6. The life in a tide pool comes from
   A. people
   B. eggs
   C. the ocean
   D. the rocks

7. One natural force that destroys tide pools is
   A. wind
   B. volcanoes
   C. animals
   D. the sun

8. The water in tide pools dries up from
   A. heat
   B. light
   C. waves
   D. people

9. The greatest enemy of tide pools is
   A. fish
   B. waves
   C. people
   D. mud

10. People can help the animals in the tide pools by
    A. collecting the animals
    B. leaving the animals alone
    C. drinking the water
    D. adding plants

The king of England did not allow the people in his colonies to make coins. He did not ship coins to them, either. The king did this to keep people from trading with France, Spain, and Holland. But some traders from these countries paid coins to colonists. The traders paid for goods such as hides, nails, and grain. Over time, coins became common in the colonies.

Some colonists began to spend large silver dollars from Spain. But they did not always have change for these coins. So they chopped the coins into eight pieces when they needed to make change. They called the Spanish coins *pieces of eight*. They called each piece of broken coin a *bit*. Four bits were worth half a dollar. Two bits were worth a quarter of a dollar. Even today the term *two bits* means a quarter of a dollar.

_____ **1.** The English king didn't allow the colonists to
  A. make coins   **C.** spend money
  B. save money   **D.** move to Spain

_____ **2.** Some traders paid coins to colonists for goods such as
  A. ships   **C.** silver
  B. hides   **D.** clothing

_____ **3.** Colonists chopped Spanish silver dollars into
  A. two pieces   **C.** six pieces
  B. four pieces   **D.** eight pieces

_____ **4.** They called each piece
  A. a quarter   **C.** a coin
  B. a bit   **D.** a dollar

_____ **5.** Four bits were worth
  A. half a dollar   **C.** a quarter of a dollar
  B. a penny   **D.** six pieces of eight

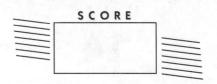
The French people who settled in Canada faced a different problem. French soldiers stationed there had to be paid regularly. The French king shipped money from France to pay them. But the French ships were often delayed by bad weather or were lost. Sometimes they were robbed by pirates.

The governor of the French colony was in charge of paying the soldiers. By 1685 money was so scarce that he had to take action. So he asked for packs of playing cards. He signed the back of each card. Then he wrote a value on each one. He paid his men with this playing card money. These cards were some of the first paper money in North America. They stayed in use for seventy years.

_____ **6.** In Canada money was
    A. not needed   **C.** in short supply
    B. easy to spend   **D.** plentiful

_____ **7.** To receive their pay on time, French soldiers in Canada depended on
    A. the king of Spain   **C.** good weather
    B. each other   **D.** the king of England

_____ **8.** Ships carrying money to the soldiers often arrived
    A. on time   **C.** early
    B. late   **D.** every week

_____ **9.** The first paper money in North America was made by
    A. a king   **C.** a soldier
    B. a pirate   **D.** a governor

_____ **10.** Playing card money was used for
    A. many years   **C.** a week
    B. a month   **D.** a day

The next time you clean out your attic, keep an eye out for old comic books. Collectors might pay a lot for any comic books you find. You may even want to start your own collection.

Collectors know just what to look for in a comic book. For instance, they always check the date first. They like to find books that came out between 1938 and 1945. These years marked the "Golden Age" of comic books. Now these books are priced very high. The first copy of Marvel Comics cost a dime when it came out. Today it sells for as much as $15,000.

Collectors also look for books in which a character appears for the first time. The first Superman story tells how Superman came to Earth. In it he claimed that he could run "faster than an express train." This comic book might cost as much as $7,500.

_____ **1.** Collectors first check a comic book's
    A. date   **C.** cover
    B. main character   **D.** author

_____ **2.** The Golden Age of comic books was
    A. before 1938   **C.** between 1938 and 1945
    B. after 1945   **D.** between 1945 and 1955

_____ **3.** Comic books from the Golden Age are now
    A. new   **C.** made of gold
    B. high-priced   **D.** unpopular

_____ **4.** The first copy of Marvel Comics cost
    A. $15,000   **C.** a dime
    B. a nickel   **D.** $7,500

_____ **5.** The first Superman story tells how Superman
    A. met Lois Lane   **C.** destroyed another planet
    B. came to Earth   **D.** flew above buildings

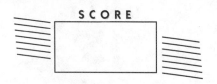
Sometimes a character from one comic book turns up in another one. When Batman is shown in a Superman comic, the price of the book goes up. These books are called crossover books. They are worth more because there are not many of them.

Don't let the high prices keep you from starting a collection of your own. Comic books that came out after the Golden Age don't cost as much. Today's comic books are even cheaper. You can enjoy them now and save them for their future value.

If you start a collection of your own, be sure to take special care of your books. Comic books are made from cheap paper. Protect them by keeping them in a dark place in special plastic bags. The newer a comic book looks, the more money it will be worth. Torn or missing pages and faded colors will lower its value.

_____ **6.** A Superman comic that shows Batman will
    A. be unpopular   **C.** cost a dime
    B. cost $7,500   **D.** be valuable

_____ **7.** In crossover comic books, two main characters meet
    A. in a distant land   **C.** in battle
    B. other friends   **D.** in the same book

_____ **8.** Collectors will pay less for comic books
    A. published in 1943   **C.** with faded pictures
    B. in plastic bags   **D.** with a new character

_____ **9.** Comic books are made from
    A. butcher paper   **C.** cheap paper
    B. tracing paper   **D.** wax paper

_____ **10.** Comic books last longest when stored in
    A. cardboard boxes   **C.** attics
    B. plastic bags   **D.** sunny rooms

The first step in making a toy is designing it. Toy designers are people who have the ideas for new toys. They work in offices or in their own homes. But they have to do more than just think of new ideas. They also have to know what young people like. An idea for a simple pull toy or building blocks is not enough. Toy designers must make the idea fit the trends of the day.

After toys are designed, samples go to "toy laboratories" for testing. There toys are pushed, pulled, and crashed by the experts—young children. Toy makers take note of what they see at the labs. They sit behind one-way mirrors. They watch children ride wheel toys and build towns with blocks. Some keep an eye out for toys that break and toys that don't work. Others make notes about how often a toy is chosen for play.

_____ **1.** The first step in making a toy is
  A. testing its safety   **C.** being sure that it works
  B. designing it   **D.** advertising it

_____ **2.** A toy designer might design toys
  A. at home   **C.** in a toy store
  B. in a school   **D.** in a lab

_____ **3.** The experts in a toy lab are
  A. children   **C.** toy makers
  B. advertising people   **D.** sales people

_____ **4.** Toy makers at labs keep an eye out for toys
  A. used for building   **C.** that don't work
  B. with wheels   **D.** that are colorful

_____ **5.** Toy makers at a toy lab might count how often
  A. children smile   **C.** one-way mirrors break
  B. they take notes   **D.** a toy is chosen

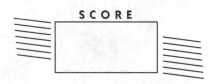

Testing for safety is another step in making toys. People in charge of toy safety work with special equipment. Their job changes with each toy they test. They might check the strength of a toy that will bear a child's weight. Or they might make sure that toys for young children don't have small pieces.

The last two steps in making toys are packaging and advertising them. Toy makers know that children like colorful objects. So they design bright packages for the toys. Writers think of catchy names for the toys. They hope children remember the names when they shop. With these steps completed, the toys are sent to toy stores. There children decide whether or not a toy becomes a big seller.

_____ **6.** Toys must be tested for
    A. color   **C.** cost
    B. safety   **D.** brightness

_____ **7.** People who check toy safety use
    A. one-way mirrors   **C.** bright packages
    B. special equipment   **D.** young children

_____ **8.** Toys for young children can't have
    A. blocks   **C.** wheels
    B. balls   **D.** small parts

_____ **9.** Toy makers know that colorful packages
    A. are liked by children   **C.** are cheap
    B. are assembled easily   **D.** last a long time

_____ **10.** The people who think of catchy names for toys are
    A. children   **C.** writers
    B. teachers   **D.** designers

Starfish of different sizes and colors live in the oceans. Starfish are often yellow, orange, or brown. But they can be bright colors, too. From point to point, a starfish can be as small as a paper clip or as long as a yardstick. Most starfish are shaped like stars, with five arms extending from their bodies. But some starfish, called sunstars, have a dozen arms. Other types have 25 arms.

Rows of tiny spines cover the top of a starfish's arms. Each spine moves easily when it is touched. Enemies that brush against a starfish may get a surprise. Some starfish spines are very sharp and have poison in them.

Underneath each arm of a starfish are rows of tiny holes. Tube feet extend from these holes. The tube feet can become suction cups to help starfish move. These suction cups hold starfish very strongly. Even storm waves will not tear a starfish from a rock.

_____ **1.** Starfish are often
   A. red   **C.** blue
   B. yellow   **D.** green

_____ **2.** From point to point, a starfish can be the size of a
   A. grain of rice   **C.** yardstick
   B. car   **D.** door

_____ **3.** A starfish can protect itself with its
   A. tube feet   **C.** mouth
   B. arms   **D.** spines

_____ **4.** The tube feet of a starfish are located
   A. on its back   **C.** under suction cups
   B. near its mouth   **D.** underneath its arms

_____ **5.** The suction cup feet of a starfish
   A. are weak   **C.** are very strong
   B. have bristles   **D.** have pointed tips

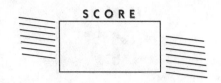
A starfish's mouth is on its underside. It is in the middle of its body. Starfish swallow small animals whole. Sometimes they eat mollusks. These include clams and oysters, which are protected by hard shells. A starfish attaches its tube feet to each side of the shell. Then it slowly pries the shell open. The starfish next pushes its stomach out through its mouth, into the open shell. There, its stomach begins to digest the soft flesh.

Fishers who collect oysters and clams sometimes try to kill starfish by cutting them into pieces. But this does not kill them. Starfish can grow new arms. They can even grow a new body. This can happen when one arm remains attached to a piece of the old body. So even a small part of a starfish's body can become another starfish.

_____ **6.** A starfish's mouth is
    A. on one arm   **C.** on its tube feet
    B. inside its stomach   **D.** on its underside

_____ **7.** Starfish swallow
    A. small animals   **C.** plants
    B. other starfish   **D.** tiny spines

_____ **8.** Oysters and clams are
    A. mammals   **C.** reptiles
    B. seashells   **D.** mollusks

_____ **9.** An oyster has
    A. a shell   **C.** arms
    B. a clam   **D.** spines

_____ **10.** If a starfish loses an arm, it will
    A. die   **C.** grow another
    B. not move   **D.** lose another

On September 30, 1492, sailors on three ships, the *Pinta*, the *Niña*, and the *Santa María,* were worried. They had left the shores of Spain weeks before. No one knew what lay ahead. They hoped for a safe voyage across the vast ocean. They also hoped that they would see land soon. But land was nowhere in sight.

Then their luck changed. They began to notice signs of land. First they saw a large flock of birds flying overhead. They even heard the birds call out. Then the crew of the *Pinta* spotted green reeds floating in the water.

Sailors on the other ships began to see signs of land, too. Those on the *Niña* saw a stick covered with barnacles. Barnacles are shellfish that grow on rocks and the bottoms of boats. The sailors began to have more hope.

_____ **1.** The ships had sailed from the shores of
- **A.** England
- **B.** France
- **C.** Spain
- **D.** Holland

_____ **2.** Sailors on all three ships hoped
- **A.** to go home
- **B.** for a safe voyage
- **C.** for rain
- **D.** for their families

_____ **3.** The sailors thought the birds had come from
- **A.** another ship
- **B.** a cage
- **C.** land
- **D.** Spain

_____ **4.** Green reeds were spotted by the crew of
- **A.** the *Pinta*
- **B.** the *Santa María*
- **C.** the *Niña*
- **D.** all three ships

_____ **5.** When the sailors saw a stick with barnacles, they felt
- **A.** better
- **B.** worried
- **C.** calm
- **D.** sad

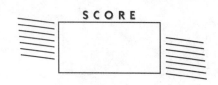
Christopher Columbus was the leader of the group. He urged the crew to be more watchful than ever. He asked that they fire a cannon when they spotted land.

Then, at ten o'clock at night on October 11, Columbus saw a light. But Columbus did not trust his own senses. He knew his strong desire to reach land might be causing his imagination to run wild. So he asked two other men if they saw the light. The first man claimed to see the light. But the second one did not.

The moon rose before midnight and lit the water. With their eyes scanning the water, the sailors on all three ships watched silently. Two hours later everyone heard the blast of a cannon. The men on the *Pinta* had seen land. All the men cheered.

_____ **6.** The crew fired a cannon when they saw
    A. a bird   **C.** the moon
    B. a candle   **D.** land

_____ **7.** Columbus saw a light
    A. before midnight   **C.** at midnight
    B. at dawn   **D.** at dusk

_____ **8.** When he saw a light, Columbus asked two men to
    A. look for it   **C.** fire the cannon
    B. go to bed   **D.** cheer

_____ **9.** When the moon rose, it
    A. surprised them   **C.** went behind clouds
    B. lit the water   **D.** looked like a candle

_____ **10.** The men who heard the cannon's blast
    A. saw a light   **C.** went to bed
    B. were happy   **D.** saw birds

Ip hangs three hundred feet above the floor of the dark cave. To reach this place, he climbed a bamboo structure built many years before. He cuts a small object off the wall of the cave. He stuffs it into a burlap bag. There is nothing to protect him from a fall. But Ip does not think of safety. He thinks only of one thing. He wonders how many more swiftlet nests he can gather before the end of the day.

For fifteen hundred years, people like Ip have risked their lives to gather nests of swiftlets. These tiny birds build nests deep inside caves. The caves often have many long and winding tunnels. Some swiftlets fly two miles inside a cave to find a safe place for a nest. Others build nests hundreds of feet above the ground on the ceiling.

_____ 1. To reach his place in the cave, Ip climbed
    A. a wall   C. ropes
    B. a ladder   D. a bamboo structure

_____ 2. Ip uses a burlap bag to
    A. protect himself   C. hold nests
    B. hold his lunch   D. hold a special tool

_____ 3. To keep from falling, Ip uses
    A. nothing   C. a bamboo structure
    B. a rope   D. a burlap bag

_____ 4. People have gathered swiftlet nests for
    A. two years   C. three hundred years
    B. one thousand years   D. fifteen hundred years

_____ 5. Swiftlets build their nests in caves that have
    A. wide doors   C. tall trees
    B. open windows   D. long tunnels

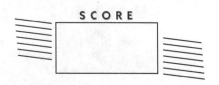
Swiftlet nests are used to make a soup called bird's nest soup. The dish is made by blending the nests with a rich chicken stock. People in Hong Kong eat a hundred tons of nests each year. There, a bowl of bird's nest soup costs about fifty dollars. Nest gathering provides a good living for Ip.

But Ip does not gather nests just for money. Nest gathering is a tradition. Fathers teach their sons the skills needed for the job. They begin climbing when they are young boys. Many climb after they are grandparents.

Old customs are also passed from father to son. Nest gatherers use a special tool to scrape nests from the caves. It is called a rada. No climber would use a different tool. And gatherers place food at the mouths of the caves. They believe that the food and the radas protect them as they climb.

_____ 6. Swiftlet nests are used to make
  A. medicine   C. bird cages
  B. soup   D. glue

_____ 7. One reason Ip gathers nests is
  A. to earn money   C. for the thrill
  B. for fun   D. to see birds

_____ 8. Many young boys learn to gather nests from
  A. their fathers   C. people in Hong Kong
  B. the swiftlets   D. teachers

_____ 9. A rada is a kind of
  A. soup   C. bird
  B. cave   D. tool

_____ 10. Gatherers place food
  A. inside nests   C. at the mouths of caves
  B. on the rada   D. inside caves

Ed lives right outside a small town. He has decided to turn his back yard into a water garden with ponds and waterfalls. He wants flowers to grow everywhere, even in the ponds. But because Ed does not know how to begin, he signs up for a tour with his neighbor, Mr. Hall. Mr. Hall is known for his water gardens. He gives tours each Saturday.

On Saturday Mr. Hall greets Ed and takes him through a gate to his gardens. They pass a pond covered with large, green leaves floating on top of the water. Mr. Hall calls them lily pads. To Ed they look like big stepping stones. Mr. Hall tells Ed about a type of water lily in South America with even bigger leaves. Its leaves can be more than five feet across. Mr. Hall explains that the plant is called the Victoria lily. Its leaves look like giant green pie pans because their edges turn up.

1. Ed and Mr. Hall live
   A. in different states   C. on different farms
   B. in the same area   D. in a large city

2. Mr. Hall gives tours
   A. every day   C. on Saturdays
   B. on Mondays   D. once a month

3. To Ed the lily pads look like
   A. green frogs   C. pie pans
   B. stones to walk on   D. waterfalls

4. The Victoria lily
   A. has enormous leaves   C. grows on land
   B. blooms each Saturday   D. has purple berries

5. The Victoria lily's leaves look like pie pans because of their
   A. size   C. name
   B. color   D. shape

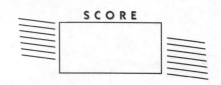
Ed sees blue flowers scattered among the leaves. The blooms stand above the water on stout stalks. Each one has several petals attached to the stem. Mr. Hall explains that these Australian water lilies bloom all day. But other types of water lilies bloom only at night. He also explains that water lilies are not always blue. They can be yellow, pink, or red.

Ed asks if the plants have roots like other flowers. Mr. Hall explains how lilies grow. He says that the fruit of each water lily is like a berry. The berries are filled with seeds. Often the fruit ripens underwater. Then the seeds float away or sink. The roots of the plants grow from the seeds.

When Ed leaves, he thanks Mr. Hall. He tells Mr. Hall that he will plant water lilies in his garden. Mr. Hall shakes Ed's hand and offers to help him. He starts by giving Ed a package of seeds.

_____ **6.** The bloom that Ed sees is
    A. blue   **C.** red
    B. yellow   **D.** pink

_____ **7.** Australian water lilies
    A. make vines   **C.** bloom all day
    B. are white   **D.** don't have roots

_____ **8.** The fruit of each water lily is like a
    A. flower   **C.** stalk
    B. berry   **D.** seed

_____ **9.** The fruit of a water lily ripens
    A. in the mud   **C.** in the spring
    B. near the petals   **D.** underwater

_____ **10.** When Ed leaves, Mr. Hall gives him
    A. stems   **C.** seeds
    B. roots   **D.** flowers

On a clear night, thousands of stars shine overhead. Billions more are too far away to see. Although they look like diamonds, they are really huge balls of gas and dust. Heat and light come from the hot centers of the stars. The light makes the stars shine. Like the billions of people on Earth, each star is unique.

The star nearest Earth is 93 million miles away. This star is our sun. It takes the sun's light eight minutes to reach Earth. Plants and animals need the light and the heat of the sun's rays to stay alive. There would be no life on Earth without the sun.

Our sun is a yellowish-white star. Other stars can be blue-white, orange, or red. The blue-white stars look as if they would be cool to the touch. But they are really the hottest. The red stars are the coolest stars.

_____ **1.** Stars are like people because each one is

     A. cold   **C.** unique

     B. bright   **D.** white

_____ **2.** The sun's light reaches Earth

     A. instantly   **C.** in eight hours

     B. within minutes   **D.** within days

_____ **3.** Without the sun, plants and animals would

     A. die   **C.** need more air

     B. grow   **D.** need more water

_____ **4.** Our sun is

     A. blue-white   **C.** yellowish-white

     B. orange   **D.** red

_____ **5.** Blue-white stars are

     A. closest to Earth   **C.** coolest

     B. hard to see   **D.** hottest

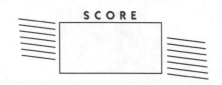
Stars also differ in brightness and size. The amount of gas and dust in a star determines if it is bright or dim. The more gas and dust a star contains, the brighter and hotter it will be. Since the bright, hot stars contain the most material, they are the largest.

Our sun is one hundred times larger than Earth. But it is only a medium-size star. The brightest, hottest stars are twenty times larger. They are called blue giants. Red dwarfs are stars that are smaller than our sun. These stars are the most common in the night sky.

Whether a star is a blue giant or a red dwarf, it is always in motion. Stars are held together by gravity. But at the same time, energy produced inside the stars tries to blow them apart. New stars form while others die. Some die by collapsing. Others explode.

_____

_____ **6.** The brightness of a star depends on its
    A. size   **C.** distance from Earth
    B. motion   **D.** distance from the sun

_____ **7.** The largest stars
    A. are orange   **C.** have cool centers
    B. are dim and cool   **D.** have more gas and dust

_____ **8.** Compared to Earth, the sun is
    A. smaller   **C.** ten times larger
    B. the same size   **D.** one hundred times larger

_____ **9.** Red dwarfs are
    A. easy to see   **C.** very large
    B. hard to see   **D.** pink

_____ **10.** Stars are held together by
    A. gas   **C.** heat
    B. dust   **D.** gravity

George Putnam

George Putnam grew up surrounded by wealth. His family owned a publishing company in New York. All the members of his family had gone to college in Boston. But after high school George made up his own mind. He went to college in California. His family was shocked. A few years later, they had an even bigger surprise. George did not join the family business.

George wanted to prove that he could do things by himself. He had three hundred dollars. He traveled to Oregon. He settled in a town named Bend. After a few years, he became editor of the newspaper. He also became mayor of the town. He left Bend to fight in World War I. Only after the war did he consider going back to New York. His father and brother had died. He sensed there would be a new challenge in the family business.

_____ **1.** George's family owned a
  A. college   C. newspaper
  B. publishing company   D. town

_____ **2.** George's family's business was located in
  A. New York   C. California
  B. Boston   D. Oregon

_____ **3.** George's family members went to college in
  A. California   C. Boston
  B. New York   D. Bend

_____ **4.** George went to Oregon to
  A. go to college   C. fight in World War I
  B. join his family   D. prove himself

_____ **5.** George left Bend to become
  A. a mayor   C. a pilot
  B. an editor   D. a soldier

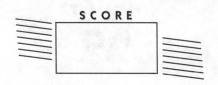

Back in New York, George worked at G. P. Putnam's Sons. He was also interested in exploring new lands. He began writing books about exploring. He led trips to Greenland and the Arctic.

In 1928 he joined some business partners. They sponsored a flight across the Atlantic Ocean. The group wanted to find a woman pilot to make the trip. They asked Amelia Earhart to go. She became the first woman to fly across the Atlantic Ocean.

George fell in love with this young pilot. He asked her to marry him. She turned him down. She did not want to get married. But George would not give up. He asked her again and again. He did not give up easily. The sixth time he asked her, she accepted. George and Amelia were married in 1931.

_____ **6.** George wrote books about
- **A.** business
- **B.** planes and pilots
- **C.** traveling to new places
- **D.** going to college

_____ **7.** George led trips to
- **A.** the Atlantic
- **B.** the Arctic
- **C.** New York
- **D.** Oregon

_____ **8.** George sponsored a flight across the Atlantic in
- **A.** 1928
- **B.** 1931
- **C.** 1982
- **D.** World War I

_____ **9.** George's partners wanted to find a woman who was
- **A.** a writer
- **B.** a flier
- **C.** an explorer
- **D.** an editor

_____ **10.** The woman George fell in love with was a
- **A.** teacher
- **B.** banker
- **C.** pilot
- **D.** mayor

The Civil War had ended at last. George, a young freed slave, stood in an apple orchard in Missouri. He was seven years old, and he lived with a German farmer and the farmer's wife. As he breathed the perfume of the trees, the sun warmed his skin. Then he noticed something that worried him. Insects swarmed inside the limbs of one of the trees. He knew the harvest would be ruined if the bugs weren't stopped.

George had a problem. He had never been able to speak clearly. He did not know how he could explain the threat to Farmer Carver. And the farmer would not be able to see the insects because they were inside the tree's limbs. Even though George couldn't speak, he had been born with a special awareness of nature. He knew the bugs were there.

_____ **1.** The story occurs right after
- **A.** World War I
- **C.** the Civil War
- **B.** World War II
- **D.** the Revolutionary War

_____ **2.** The apple trees in the story were
- **A.** along a road
- **C.** in a field
- **B.** near a valley
- **D.** in an orchard

_____ **3.** George was
- **A.** seven
- **C.** an old man
- **B.** six
- **D.** a teenager

_____ **4.** George looked at an apple tree and knew insects were
- **A.** on the leaves
- **C.** in the apples
- **B.** inside the limbs
- **D.** in the roots

_____ **5.** When George noticed the insects, he felt
- **A.** happy
- **C.** worried
- **B.** sad
- **D.** relaxed

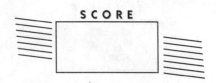
George led Farmer Carver to the sick tree. "What do you want? I can't understand you," the farmer said. He went back to work. George sighed. He then tried to tell Frau Carver. Of all the people George knew, she best understood his special language. But she just looked puzzled as he made sounds and pointed at the tree.

George got a saw and began to saw off the bad branches. Farmer Carver raced to him. He shouted angrily, "Stop! What are you doing?" George ran to Frau Carver. He tried to speak, but she still couldn't understand him.

Frau Carver knew George was trying to say something important. She looked at the branch in his hand and gasped. Then she and Farmer Carver both saw the tiny insects crawling on the branch. George, who later was known as Dr. George Washington Carver, had saved the apple harvest.

_____ 6. George's special language was understood by
  A. Farmer Carver   C. a neighbor
  B. a teacher   D. Frau Carver

_____ 7. To cut the branches off the tree, George used
  A. a saw   C. a hatchet
  B. an ax   D. a knife

_____ 8. The farmer saw George cut the branch, so he
  A. gasped   C. went back to work
  B. called Frau Carver D. shouted

_____ 9. Frau Carver looked at the cut branch and saw
  A. insects   C. buds
  B. the ax   D. an apple

_____ 10. This story is about the childhood of
  A. Farmer Carver   C. George Washington
  B. George W. Carver   D. Frau Carver

Millions of cattle roamed on the open range in the Old West. Cattle ranchers rounded them up. They could sell them in Texas for four or five dollars each. But Easterners also liked to eat beef. They would pay from forty to fifty dollars each. So cattle ranchers hired cowboys to drive their cattle north. In towns like Abilene and Dodge City, the railroads crossed the plains. There the cattle were put on trains headed for the East Coast.

Before each trail drive, several ranchers hired a leader for the long trip. This trail boss hired ten to twelve cowboys to round up the cattle. While the roundup was going on, the trail boss hired a wrangler and a cook. The wrangler gathered fifty or more horses for the trip. The cook prepared the chuck wagon for cooking beans, bacon, and biscuits on the trail.

_____ **1.** A cow could be sold in Texas for
  A. ten dollars   **C.** forty dollars
  B. four dollars   **D.** fifty dollars

_____ **2.** Cattle were driven
  A. east   **C.** north
  B. west   **D.** south

_____ **3.** Cattle were taken to the East Coast on
  A. horses   **C.** wagons
  B. trains   **D.** trucks

_____ **4.** The leader of a trail drive was called a
  A. trail boss   **C.** cook
  B. wrangler   **D.** roundup

_____ **5.** Before the trail drive, the cook prepared the
  A. horses   **C.** cattle
  B. saddles   **D.** chuck wagon

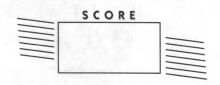

Each trail drive lasted for two or three months. The cowboys drove the cattle as far as one thousand miles. They moved from two thousand to three thousand cattle on each drive. Those who were new to the job rode behind the herd. The dust clogged their throats and burned their eyes. At night some cowboys circled the herd, often singing to pass the time. Others slept next to saddled horses, ready for action.

Cowboys faced thieves, storms, and unfriendly tribes on trail drives. But they feared stampedes the most. If a single cow was startled and ran, all the others followed. The earth shook with a deafening roar under their pounding hooves. After one stampede, the restless cattle were easily scared into stampeding again. Cowboys knew that they couldn't stop a stampeding herd. But they rode in front of it and tried to turn the cattle into a circle. This did not always help. Herds sometimes ran for days.

_____ **6.** Trail drives lasted
    A. two or three months **C.** two or three days
    B. two or three years   **D.** two or three weeks

_____ **7.** At times the number of cattle on a drive was
    A. twelve   **C.** one thousand
    B. fifty   **D.** three thousand

_____ **8.** On the trail new cowboys were positioned
    A. in front of the herd **C.** next to the herd
    B. behind the herd   **D.** among the herd

_____ **9.** On the trail a cowboy slept ready for
    A. rain   **C.** coffee
    B. action   **D.** a bath

_____ **10.** Stampedes were caused by
    A. horses   **C.** a frightened animal
    B. a sick animal   **D.** singing cowboys

The California sun streamed in the window. Yoshiko gazed at her mother's face. Her mother was a poet. She was reading a *tanka*. A tanka is a Japanese poem with 31 syllables. Yoshiko listened to the calm voice. She closed her eyes. She did not want to miss a single beat of the verse.

Yoshiko's parents had grown up in Japan. They had moved to California before Yoshiko was born. They wanted her to know about the Japanese culture. So her family read Japanese stories and books. They wrote and received letters from Japan. Guests from Japan came to their home. When she was ten, Yoshiko began writing her own stories. These stories marked the start of her life as a writer.

_____ 1. Yoshiko and her parents lived in
  A. Japan   C. Boston
  B. California   D. Tokyo

_____ 2. Yoshiko's mother was a
  A. cook   C. musician
  B. doctor   D. poet

_____ 3. A tanka is a special
  A. story   C. poem
  B. song   D. letter

_____ 4. Yoshiko learned about Japan from
  A. television   C. her parents
  B. school   D. a neighbor

_____ 5. Yoshiko wrote her first stories when she was
  A. ten   C. fifteen
  B. twelve   D. twenty

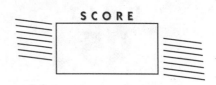
Yoshiko's work reflects her life as a Japanese American. Her first book, *The Dancing Kettle*, retells some folk tales of Japan. She thinks that folk tales tell about feelings that all humans share. She hopes the tales will help people see that they have many of the same hopes and fears.

Yoshiko has written many other stories. Some are picture books for young children. Another tells about the first settlers from Japan. Other books tell about growing up in California. These are titled *A Jar of Dreams* and *The Best Bad Thing*.

Yoshiko's books give today's young Japanese Americans something new. It is something that she did not have when she was young. Few people had written books about being Japanese in America. Her books are among the first that blend the two cultures.

_____ **6.** Yoshiko's first book is called
    A. *The First Settlers*   **C.** *The Best Bad Thing*
    B. *The Dancing Kettle*   **D.** *A Jar of Dreams*

_____ **7.** Yoshiko thinks that folk tales tell about
    A. feelings   **C.** growing up
    B. settlers   **D.** Japan

_____ **8.** Yoshiko has written
    A. a comedy   **C.** a picture book
    B. a journal   **D.** for the newspaper

_____ **9.** Yoshiko wrote about
    A. Japanese Americans   **C.** famous writers
    B. young girls   **D.** Californians

_____ **10.** Books about the blending of two cultures are
    A. common   **C.** old
    B. hard   **D.** new

Ancient Cities

Human beings have probably lived on the earth about two million years. But they have lived in towns and cities for only about ten thousand years. These cities grew from small farming villages. Over time, farming methods improved. Extra food was grown and stored. More and more people stopped farming and moved to towns. There they learned a skill or worked in shops. Some worked for the government.

The first cities appeared in what is now Iraq about 3500 B.C. They were built next to rivers in a great valley. People lived close to the rivers because they had to carry water to their homes. Because of this, towns could not be spread out over large areas. Most towns covered less than a square mile. High walls circled many towns. Other towns were built on hills.

_____ **1.** Human beings have lived in towns and cities for about
   A. two million years   **C.** one thousand years
   B. five hundred years   **D.** ten thousand years

_____ **2.** Some people who lived in ancient towns worked
   A. as farmers   **C.** as garbage collectors
   B. for the government   **D.** for Iraq

_____ **3.** The first cities appeared in Iraq about
   A. 3500 B.C.   **C.** 1435 B.C.
   B. 200 B.C.   **D.** one thousand years ago

_____ **4.** The first cities were built next to
   A. forts   **C.** rivers
   B. forests   **D.** prairies

_____ **5.** Many early towns were circled by
   A. water   **C.** hills
   B. walls   **D.** homes

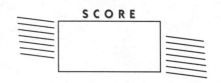

If you could visit an ancient city, you would first be drawn to the town center. There you would see a grand palace. This was the home of the ruler and his family. People would rush past you on their way to work in large government buildings. You would see shops lining the crowded streets. Next you might pass a temple where people gather for prayer. Or you might stroll past a market. There you could see farmers selling fruits and grains or people buying cloth and candles. If you walked away from the center of town, you might see huge warehouses. These were used for storing grains and weapons.

Leaving the town center, you would walk down narrow dirt streets. You'd notice small houses crowded together. But you'd have to step carefully. People in early towns threw their garbage in the streets or piled it outside the town walls. And after a hard rain, the streets were clogged with mud for several days.

_____ **6.** Early leaders lived
    A. outside the cities   **C.** in town centers
    B. in small houses   **D.** near farming villages

_____ **7.** People gathered at the market to
    A. grow fruit   **C.** learn a skill
    B. pray   **D.** buy things

_____ **8.** Warehouses were full of
    A. fruits   **C.** cloth
    B. grains   **D.** candles

_____ **9.** People in ancient cities put their trash in
    A. the streets   **C.** dumps
    B. bags   **D.** warehouses

_____ **10.** The streets of ancient cities were made of
    A. dirt   **C.** rocks
    B. stone   **D.** grains

Fact Finding

Study the building directory below. Use the facts to answer the questions.

BUILDING DIRECTORY

Al's Advertising Agency......................4th Floor

Dentist..1st Floor

The Flower Cart ....1st Floor

Haircuts by Paula ....2nd Floor

Housewares Magazine ....3rd Floor

Kramer's Travel Agency....................2nd Floor

Lincoln Employment Agency...............3rd Floor

Osgood and Osgood, Lawyers ....5th Floor

---

1. You have a toothache. What floor will you go to?

_____

2. You are planning a vacation. What agency will you visit?

_____

3. What two businesses are on the third floor?

_____

4. You need a haircut. Which business would you use?

_____

5. What two businesses each take up a whole floor?

_____

Traveling Facts

Answer these fact questions about travel. Use complete sentences. Use the word box to find your answers. You may use more than one word for each answer.

airplane	automobile	boat	bus
canoe	ferry	helicopter	jet
money	suitcase	ticket	train

1. What are some ways to travel by land?

_____

_____

2. What are some ways to travel by water?

_____

_____

3. What are some ways to travel by air?

_____

_____

4. What are some things you might need when traveling?

_____

_____

To check your answers, turn to page 62.

Just the Facts, Please!

Newspaper reporters give facts in their stories. They try to answer six main questions. **Who** was involved? **What** happened? **When** did it happen? **Where** did it happen? **Why** did it happen? **How** did it happen?

Pretend you are a reporter for a newspaper. Write a story about a big storm in your town. In your story try to answer the six questions.

Giant Storm Hits Town!

_____

_____

_____

_____

_____

_____

_____

_____

_____

_____

_____

_____

_____